Praise for Jennifer's
Memoir Writing Workshops:

"Many, many thanks for an amazing weekend. It was worth every minute of traveling....I will be forever grateful and in remembrance of the incredible women in this group!"

— PS, San Francisco CA

"Thanks so much to Jennifer for leading us on a rich, evocative journey."

— ZR, Lee MA

"Jennifer's passion for 'women who write' is evident in her ongoing commitment to those of us who do. In a soft voice she fearlessly leads, directs, and most of all...deeply cares. We wrote from our hearts and she opened hers, steering us here, guiding us there and always... leading us right back to ourselves."

— NP, Dallas TX

"Thank you for encouraging and nurturing us to tell our life stories. I was at first intimidated by those in the group who were so much farther along than I, but our sharing sessions have given me more confidence and empowered me to continue chronicling my family's journey (and mine along with it)."

— MS, Washington DC

"Jennifer provided a warm and accepting safe haven for us to share the tender parts of ourselves through writing exercises presented with an expert and delicate hand. The format kept us moving, thinking, laughing, writing, and the time flew! At the end of this weekend, I felt both inspired and encouraged that, maybe, just maybe, I really can write!"

— AS, Lenox MA

THE ELEMENTAL JOURNEY OF
PURPOSEFUL MEMOIR

A WRITER'S COMPANION

JENNIFER BROWDY

Green
Fire
Press

Housatonic
Massachusetts

Cover photo by Jennifer Browdy
Cover and page design by Anna Myers Sabatini

Library of Congress Control Number: 2016912085
ISBN: 978-0-9861980-5-2   978-0-9861980-6-9

Green
Fire
Press

Green Fire Press
PO Box 377 Housatonic MA 01236

For my writing companions Diane and Grace

Contents

THE ELEMENTAL JOURNEY OF
PURPOSEFUL MEMOIR

A WRITER'S
COMPANION

INTRODUCTION

Embarking on the Elemental Journey of Purposeful Memoir

Embarking on the Elemental Journey of Purposeful Memoir

f you are reading this book, you have probably been mulling over stories from your life that you would like to capture in writing—for yourself, your loved ones, and perhaps for broader audiences as well. I am here to encourage you to take this urge seriously, and to offer you guidance on what I call the elemental journey of purposeful memoir, using the four elements—Earth, Water, Fire and Air—as a structuring framework.

Purposeful memoir asks you to look back in order to move forward more confidently and courageously; to consider how your personal history has played out against the larger dramas of the political and planetary spheres; to lay claim to your intentions and values; and to consider how you can use your gifts and talents to make the world a more vibrant place for yourself and others.

In writing my own memoir, *What I Forgot...And Why I Remembered*, it wasn't until late in the process of writing that I realized my larger purpose. Trying to understand how and why I had been tossed up on some rocky, treacherous shoals as an adult, I began by simply writing disconnected scenes from my childhood and young adulthood, focusing on moments that had imprinted themselves indelibly in my memory. Slowly I began to see patterns emerging from the warp and woof of my experience, and gradually I recognized how my individual life had been played out against a social and environmental backdrop of which I was often only barely aware. As I patiently worked away, accumulating piles of written memories, the "backdrop" began to assert itself more and more, until I realized that my purpose in writing was to show how tightly we individual humans are connected to each other and to the planet that sustains us all, and to offer my life story as a beacon to others on the road to the sustainable future I am passionate about creating.

Just as no two lives are the same, each memoir will be different. The purpose I came to through writing memoir was as unique as my own life experience. While your purpose will be uniquely yours, what remains universal is the fact that every human being is shaped and molded by the social and physical landscapes against which our individual lives play out. And all of us go through stages of life that, in my own memoir, I recognized as forming an "elemental journey": Earth, the childhood ground of our being; Water, the social currents into which we are swept as adolescents and young adults; Fire, the passions and challenges of adulthood; and Air, our constant efforts to understand and make sense of it all. Not only do the elements serve as a logical metaphorical structure for memoir, they also literally underpin our lives in ways that we are only now, in the 21st century, beginning to acknowledge more fully. Without the gracious abundance of Earth, Water, Fire and Air, we humans simply could not exist. The elemental journey of purposeful memoir invites us to take stock of both the unique and the universal in every life story, offering the specific details of our lives while exploring their larger meaning and significance for the benefit of others.

Getting started with purposeful memoir

When you begin writing purposeful memoir, you don't have to know what your memoir is "about," or why you are being called to write. You just need to make a commitment—to yourself, above all—to share your experience in a clear-eyed and open-hearted way, taking your time and focusing on the journey through memory, rather than on any given goal or destination. Especially during the first draft, it's all about the process, and whatever happens along the way is just between you and the page; it can actually be counter-productive to be too careful in the initial stages of writing. It's also best in the beginning to try to keep at bay your hopes for (or anxieties about) sharing your memoir with readers, whether family, friends or the general public. That may or may not come later. At the beginning of the project, just try to relax into your memories and write whatever comes. If you remember a particular scene from your past, you can trust that it must be lodged in your memory for a reason, given how many hours and days just vanish into the ether of lived experience without leaving a trace. The prompts in this book will help you excavate these persistent scenes fully, guiding you to explore your memories from different angles, including the larger background as well as detailing the up-close-and-personal foreground. Often it will take several approaches before you arrive at the deep vein of gold buried at the center of what may seem like an oddball memory. That aha! moment, when you finally understand why this particular scene has stayed with you, is worth a hundred hours of ho-hum writing to arrive at. Stay with it!

I have taught writing for many years—memoir, essay and journalism in the college classroom and, more recently, memoir workshops for adults. I have always found that no matter the topic or genre, the best way to start the writing process is with free-writing. Free-writing is like writing in your journal: it's off-the-cuff, off-the-record kind of writing, a way to warm up and animate your writing voice. It's also a great way to get all the extraneous chatter out of your head—the to-do lists, the mutters of resentment, the whispers of doubt. Free write them all out on the page and let them stay there while you move on to the next stage of writing, the focused free-write.

This book is full of prompts for focused free-writes. I call them catalysts rather than prompts, because my hope is that they will function as dynamic sparks for your writing, rather than mundane directions. You can't give directions when you don't know where the traveler is going, and at the outset of memoir, even you can't know exactly where you're going. You surely have some ideas, but if you stay open and let the catalysts work alchemically with your memories, you may end up quite far from your original intention—and that's good! Writing memoir is like taking a trip without a tour guide and with only the most rudimentary of maps—no GPS here! You have to be prepared for surprises, and to accept that while you are not entirely in control of the journey, it is sure to be an interesting ride. With any kind of writing, I always tell students that the most important thing is that they, the writer, should not be bored. If you're bored as you write, your reader will undoubtedly be bored too. When you're writing memoir, if you find yourself totally wrapped up in describing a scene, reliving it so completely as you write that you're suddenly sobbing or laughing out loud, bingo! You are doing your job of getting the emotional heart of the scene out on paper, and you can rest assured that this scene is telling you something that you—and your eventual readers—need to know.

With focused free-writing, there are no right or wrong words; there are no true paths or false starts; nothing is wasted or unimportant. Yes, it's true, you may end up writing three times more than you actually need, including many scenes that you would not ultimately be willing to share with the world. You may shock yourself with some of the violent, even ugly emotions that erupt from your past when you open up a channel for them to escape onto the page. Let it all out: the good and the bad, the hope and the despair, the joy, rage and sorrow...the full emotional panoply of this precious life journey you're on. Without emotion, memoir becomes little more than a résumé—a flattened out account of where you've been and what you've done. Purposeful memoir asks you to dig deeper, mining your past for the nuggets of wisdom that will help you understand your own life more fully, and relate your personal experience to the larger social narratives that have unfolded during your lifetime.

Focused free-writes, the basic building blocks of purposeful memoir, can be of any length. If you're writing alone, write until the inspiration falters, until the well of that particular scene or description runs dry. You'll be surprised at how much you can accomplish in a half-hour of writing, especially if you can get into a regular routine—a half-hour every morning, let's say, with your first cup of coffee. When I lead a memoir-writing workshop, I offer many short catalysts of 10 to 15 minutes' worth of writing. These are intended as starting points, like an initial drive-by of a given memory, to be returned to and developed more thoroughly later. Everyone's writing process is different, but I find that short focused free-writes help to overcome your inner critic, that sarcastic little editor-imp who sits on your shoulder as you write and tells you that you're not making sense, or that you have nothing to write that's worth sharing. It's very important in the early stages of writing memoir to get that imp off your shoulder and booted out the door, so that you can relax into the writing and let it flow freely. Focused free-writes are low-pressure and exploratory, as first drafts should be. You can't expect yourself to write a masterpiece in a focused free-write, although sometimes you'll be surprised at the beautiful sentences that will suddenly come through you. These are the "keepers," the sentences or phrases that you may want to use as the starting point for your next pass at a given scene; the ones that may, eventually, find their way into the first full draft of your memoir.

For yes, that is ultimately the goal: to find the through-line of your memoir, and organize into a nice tight narrative all those scenes you've written higgledy-piggledy as focused free-writes. This will take time, determination and, perhaps, the help of a good editor. But that is down the road a ways; this book is focused on the earlier stages of the journey. The catalysts beckon you to jump in and start writing, without allowing yourself to be distracted by concerns about where it's all going, how it will hang together, or what it's all for.

However, I do encourage you to entertain those kinds of questions in your process reflections. When I teach memoir, we pause for process reflections after every few sessions of writing. Here is where you can look back over your focused free-writes and wonder on paper about why that particular memory was surfacing today; why your portrait of that friend turned out to be so sour; or why you were totally unable to write about the puppy-hood of your old dog. In the process notes, you can ask lots of questions, make notes to yourself about possibilities for further elaboration or revision of a scene, and even make lists or sketches. Process notes are like the scribbles in the margins of your book-in-development. They're notes to yourself, not meant to be shared...and thus they are safe spaces where you can be completely honest. You can even let that editor-imp back in again during the process writing if you feel the need to let some of its criticism out on to the page. Just be sure, if you entertain your inner critic, that you also give time and space in your process notes to your inner *coach*, who will reassure you that even if your writing is not perfect (and what focused free-write could possibly be perfect?) it is valuable, important, and worth continuing. Take that, you editor-imp!

Giving good feedback

Learning how to give useful feedback on a draft of writing is an important skill for a writer, whether you're working alone or with others. I am including here some tried-and-true strategies for writing pairs or small groups, which you can also use by yourself, as you are always your own most important first reader. I encourage you to find some other memoirists with whom to share focused free-writes and drafts; if there are none in your neighborhood, look for opportunities for retreats, workshops or online writing communities. While much of the work of a writer is necessarily solitary, there is nothing as rewarding and invigorating as sharing your rough drafts with a thoughtful, appreciative writing partner or group.

Particularly with memoir, trust is essential. Make sure you establish at the outset your policy on confidentiality—what is shared in the room should stay in the room (this is as true for virtual rooms as for physical ones). You should also come to agreement on how you're going to respond to each other's work. The guidelines below can serve as a blueprint for giving constructive feedback that encourages the writer to think more deeply about her writing. The goal here is not to edit each other's work; this is not about "fixing" anything, giving directives or criticizing. Instead, if you follow the guidelines I've laid out, you will become accustomed to offering useful feedback that shows the writer where she is shining and gently leads her to consider where her work needs more elaboration or revision. Later in the process of book development, there will be time for more precise editing—pruning, shaping and redesigning. In the early stages, what's needed more than anything else is a writing group or partner who appreciates, nurtures and cultivates your unique creative voice—whether that voice is deeply buried, tender and shy, or rollicking and ready to rip.

Guidelines for Giving Feedback on Early Draft Writing

✳ Always read your writing out loud—to yourself or to others. There is no better way to catch things like awkward phrasing, run-on sentences, repetitive word choice or an unintended tone. If you're reading to yourself, read with a pencil in hand, and underline the words, phrases or ideas that jump out at you as you read. If you're working with a partner or group, they should take notes as you read, pointing especially to words, phrases and ideas that jumped out at them—for positive or negative reasons. If your listener asks to hear the piece aloud again, happily comply! That means they're really interested.

✳ Start with the positive, and be specific. It's not helpful to say, "That was good! I liked it." Instead, take the time and make the effort to really break down what you liked about the piece. Start by sharing the words, phrases and ideas that you underlined or wrote down, and then try to explain why they caught your attention. Whether it was because you loved the metaphor or description, or because an idea was unclear or confusing, this is the kind of feedback a writer can really use.

✳ Use the following prompts to work your way into a conversation with the writer about their work:

I heard you saying...

> "I heard you saying that your grandmother was a very important force in your life.... could you say a bit more about how she influenced you?"

I noticed...

> "I noticed that you didn't talk about your dad at all in this scene. Was he in the house at the time?"

I wonder why...

> "I wonder why you decided to begin this scene about your sister with a description

of your bedroom. Did you share the bedroom with her?"

Have you considered...

"Have you considered giving more background about the town you grew up in, and maybe making the time period a bit clearer?"

I'd like to hear more about...

"I'd like to hear more about the effect of the Great Depression on your grandparents and your parents."

Note that in each case, the prompt leads to a question that the listener poses to the writer. If the sharing session is working well, the *writer* should be doing most of the talking. It's the job of the listener to ask good, penetrating questions that get the writer to think more deeply, or differently, about her draft.

✳ Be sure to allow some time at the end of the workshop session for process writing about the issues and insights brought out during the sharing and discussion. You will want to meditate on paper about plans for elaboration or revision, making notes of questions to be explored later or research to be undertaken. You should come out of a workshop session energized and ready to continue on your journey, wherever it may lead you.

Structure and goals of this book

This book leads you on a month-by-month writing journey in the form of an intertwining quadruple-helix spiral, guiding you to explore the chronological stages of your life (Earth/Childhood, Water/Young Adulthood, Fire/Adulthood) from different perspectives, with Air, your commentary, running through it all in the form of reflections. Although the western 12-month calendar does not align precisely with the zodiac, each month not only corresponds with an astrological sign, but also with an element. It's not necessary to know these correspondences to navigate this book; but if you're interested you can consult the chart at the end of the book for more information. The journey begins in January, an Earth sign month, with a focus on childhood, and continues with writing catalysts that spiral through the year, the elements/life stages, and different aspects of your experience as an individual, a social being, and a Gaian—an inhabitant of our planet. You don't need to proceed in order, though—you can dive in anywhere, anytime. Writing is an idiosyncratic process, and you should give yourself plenty of freedom to chart your own course. Some catalysts will set off more sparks than others for you, and that's fine! You should go where the action is, and make sure you are thoroughly engaged and interested at every step of the way. If you are working through the book with a writing group, just come to agreement in advance on how you intend to proceed—month by month, element by element, or totally randomly!

The most important thing is to take your time and enjoy the journey, without worrying too much about the ultimate goal. Maybe you want to produce a publishable memoir in a year's time. Maybe you just want to get to know yourself better. No matter your initial intention, and whatever your goal or passion in life, you will find that understanding the full complexity of your past experience will give you a valuable perspective on where you are now, and help you chart a meaningful course into the future. Come now. Let's go!

Your Month-by-Month Writer's Companion:

Guidance and Catalysts for
Writing Purposeful Memoir

JANUARY

Dreaming Deep

anuary in the northern hemisphere is the dead of winter, the time of stillness, of dreaming in the dark and going deep inside ourselves for wisdom. In our electrified, screen-mediated times, we often force our way past this natural rhythm, keeping our relentless activity going no matter how dark or cold it is outside. In January, coming down from all the holiday bustle—the excitements, the disappointments, the decadence and the resolutions—we owe it to ourselves to take some time to pause and reflect on how we got to where we are today, and what paths we want to trace for ourselves in the year ahead.

For a writer, this means writing, and January is a good time for that. See if you can take advantage of the long hours of darkness, writing late at night or early in the morning when your house is quiet and you can feel the swirling creativity of the dream worlds that engulf most humans—indeed, most sentient beings—when the Earth is turned away from the sun. Tapping into the dream landscape, where anything can happen, what characters from your past await you, waving vigorously from that darkened shore, trying to attract your attention? What stories do they have to share with you—and through you, with the world?

In January, though the ice may be frozen over the stream, the water still flows beneath. Your task is to drill down through the layers that have formed between you and your childhood, surprising yourself with the memories that come rising slowly to the surface, intact with details and laden with insights that can only come with the passage of time. Start anywhere. Start where you are. Just start writing and let the words cut a trail for you, back into your past.

January Catalysts

Earth: Charting Early Childhood

s we allow the darkness of the winter solstice to guide us towards renewal and transformation, imagine you could speak in the voice of yourself as an unborn child in the secure darkness of the womb, waiting to be born. What are you hoping for as you move closer to your entry into the breathing world? If you could speak to your mother from the womb, what would you say to her? How might she answer you?

esearch what was happening in the world in the 21 months that comprise the time from your conception to the celebration of your first birthday—and more specifically, during the month leading up to the day of your birth. What was happening in the "official history" of your nation, your state, your town? How might this larger socio-political backdrop have affected your parents, particularly your mother, during your gestation and first year of life?

tarting from your birth date, describe the physical landscape into which you came forth as a newborn baby. Where on the planet did you spend your first year of life? As you came into consciousness of your surroundings, what did you notice around you, whether in the natural or the built environment? What lasting traces has this early initiation into planetary citizenship left on you?

FEBRUARY

Looking for Love

e write memoir out of love. First of all, love for ourselves. It takes a lot of devotion to one's own life to spend so much time unraveling the story of how we came to be who we are. The demon shadow of this self-love is self-indulgence, and there are some memoirs, to be sure, that fall victim to the complex of "Mirror, mirror on the wall, who's the fairest of them all?" The purposeful memoirist writes not out of vanity or the imperious demand to be admired, but rather because we know that our stories, told with love, can make a positive difference in the world.

One of Rainer Maria Rilke's poems beautifully expresses how, as a memoirist, you must become your own best "quiet friend," reaching out a hand lovingly to your earlier self to offer guidance on the bumpy journey of life. Rilke enjoins us to take the people, circumstances and events that batter us and, through the alchemy of writing, transmute the bitter dregs of experience into the sweet elixir of wine.

This February, don't settle for the thin veneer of romance that passes for Cupid's arrow on Valentine's Day. Go deeper. Who and what have you truly loved? How has your love been returned? Allow yourself to glow with the bliss of requited passion, but at the same time, don't shrink from the bitterness you may have found along the winding trails of love. All of your experience is important and meaningful. Your first task is to overcome your inner censor and let it all out on to the page. Later you can become more discerning, working to understand which characters and scenes are important to the main thread of the story that wants to come through you. Later still, during the process of revision, you will think through the hard questions of structure: where does this story begin, and where will it end? Why should I include this anecdote, but leave this other beloved memory out?

Now, in the early stages of writing purposeful memoir, think of yourself as a dog following a trail with tail-wagging enthusiasm. Everything is interesting, in part because you don't know yet where this particular trail will lead. Lovingly embrace your task of exploratory writing, and let curiosity be your guide. If a memory is rising to the surface insistently, begging to be told, let it come out onto the page. Look it in the eyes. Give it your attention. Later— much, much later—you can decide whether or not to share it with the world.

February Catalysts

Air: Reflecting on Love and Connection

veryone feels some tension between the freedom of solitude and the security of connectedness. How has this tension manifested in your life? Describe a moment when you were perfectly content to be alone. Describe another moment when you were blissfully connected to another human being or group. How have you managed to navigate between these poles in your life? Have you ever achieved the balance we all crave? If so, take us to that moment. If not, maybe now is the time to imagine, deeply, what a balanced life might be like.

n their struggles for human rights and social justice, Gandhi and Martin Luther King Jr. used the idea of "soul force" as a force that works creatively and lovingly through individuals to oppose violence and oppression. As Dr. King put it in his famous "I Have A Dream" speech, delivered on the steps of the Lincoln Memorial in Washington D.C. on August 28, 1963: "We must forever conduct our struggle on the high plane of dignity and discipline. We must not allow our creative protest to degenerate into physical violence. Again and again we must rise to the majestic heights of meeting physical force with soul force."

Looking back over your life, can you identify moments where your soul force surged through in response to challenges you faced with others, perhaps because of your identity, heritage or social affiliations? Have you ever called on soul force to strengthen your work for a cause or as an ally for others? If so, describe these moments in detail; if not, can you imagine a scenario where you might allow soul force to work through you for yourself or others? Describe, with all the truth and specificity of good speculative fiction.

ight it be possible to love places in the same way that we love people? Describe, in loving detail, a place that has made you happy. What specific features of that place delight your senses and enliven your spirit? Imagine this special place like a lover waiting impatiently for you to return, writing you tantalizing love letters that describe the sensuous and emotional embrace that awaits you. Write at least one of those letters this month.

MARCH

Sap Rising

n the northern hemisphere, March is the month when the wind blows through the treetops, and down in the roots the sap starts rising, sweetness drawn up out of the earth all the way into the tips of the trees, prompting the miraculous unfurling of brilliant green leaves. This month, cast yourself into the flow of your own emergence as a young adult, thinking back to your years as a teenager or twenty-something. As the sap of your youth rose impetuously, unstoppably, what met you as you reached out into the world? Was your creativity greeted with encouragement, or rebuffed, perhaps misunderstood? Were you aware of committing your life to a greater purpose? Or did you have the sense of being adrift on an aimless sea of disconnected experiences?

However you lived your youth, now is your time to recount what was, and to consider what might have been. Mainline us into your past by giving us bold, direct descriptions of how it was to be a young person in your time and place. Assume that even if we don't understand, we sympathize compassionately: we want to see through your eyes and live through your body. Give it to us straight. Let that creative sap rise unobstructed.

Audre Lorde famously described "the erotic" as "self-connection shared." This is your task, in writing purposeful memoir of your young adult years: to convey your own erotic power—or the way it was blocked. Just as sap can be siphoned off to feed others' purposes, your erotic life energy may have been diverted to satisfy the desires of others. However your young adulthood unfolded, now is your time to bear witness and use the nuggets of sweetness, grace and power that you find in your past to further your understanding of who you are now, and who you want to become.

Let it rip! Let it spurt! Harness the power of hindsight to boil that sap into sweet syrup. Make it yours, make it ours. Make it count.

March Catalysts

Water: Stepping out as Teenager

n the northern hemisphere, March is a moody, unpredictable time, when—weather-wise, at least—anything is possible. Write a moment—or several scenes—from your life as a teenager or early twenty-something, when you felt the heady sensation of stepping into your independence. What did you want to do with your newfound freedom? And then what happened?

ow free are we, really, to choose our life direction? As children we may believe we can accomplish all our dreams, only to discover as young adults how the social landscape into which we were born shapes and often limits us. Thinking back to your young adult years, describe a moment when you felt insight into what you wanted to do with your life—when you felt a vocation calling you. Once you had a sense of direction and purpose, what happened next?

magine Gaia as a loving mother, and humanity as her teenaged children. Slipping into Gaia's voice, write to humanity as a species, taking the present moment on the planet as a backdrop. What would Gaia want us to notice? What congratulations, admonition or advice might she have for us today? Now turn this into a dialogue: answer Gaia in your own voice, being aware as you do so of how your personal teenaged relationship with your mother might shape this interaction with Mother Earth. Continue the dialogue as long as the inspiration lasts: this could be a single exchange, or it could turn into volumes.

APRIL

Fueling the Creative Fires

here is nothing I love to do more than walk through a New England forest on a sunny morning in April, when the trees are decked out in their shiny new neon-green leaves, and the soft forest floor is crowded with unfurling fiddleheads and glistening, gaudy jack-in-the-pulpits. Birds are darting overhead, busy tending to their nests, and there is a general feeling of vibrancy as the Earth warms to the glowing embrace of the Sun. Although the rhyme says that April is the time of showers, it is also a fire month, and I encourage you to use both the cool nourishment of rain and the delicious heat of the sun to fuel your creative fires on these lively spring days. Imagine yourself as a young adult, with all the fierce drive of a seed cast into the fertile earth. Nurtured by soil, water and sunlight, the seed sprouts and pushes upward with incredible determination, growing around any obstacles in its path

to fulfill its destiny of becoming—what? A flower? A lettuce head? An ancient hemlock?

Human beings grow this way too. Of course, like every other life form on Earth, we grow best in optimal conditions. But no matter where we're planted or what we encounter, we grow the best we can, reaching for the light. This month, chart the early years of your adulthood, paying attention to signs and conditions that you may not have noticed much while you were in the heat of the moment. Who was around you and what were they doing? What were the broader societal circumstances that nourished you or held you back? What sources of inspiration were beaming down on you, lighting your path and encouraging you onward?

We know now that the soil teams with life visible only under a microscope. Turn the scope of your memory on to your early years as an adult, and see what you find there. Write as a seeker, the words an unfurling bridge of questions, leading into your past.

April Catalysts

Fire: Exploring The Passions
of Adulthood

ove springs eternal, the saying goes; meaning that even though we may experience the pain of unrequited or lost love, most of us are still willing to take the risk of falling in love again. Describe the most passionate romance you've had to date, with as much loving detail as you can muster. Take yourself back to the thrill of the early days of a new romance: the anticipation of a date, the delight of finding your interest matched by your partner, the heady joy of being in love with an adoring mate. No matter what happened later with this partner, take the time now to focus on the emotions and sensations of the magical early days and weeks of your passion. Let these memories set your mind and body alight now.

Or, if you have never yet felt the glow of requited romantic passion for another person, step bravely into the breach, and explore times in your life where you have come close, or the disappointments you've had. Take some time to think in writing about why "true love" has not yet happened for you.

hat are you truly passionate about? What causes or issues have you cared about over the course of your life, and how have they changed or remained constant over time? What are you willing to stand up and fight for today, in the fiery style of Aries the warrior? Write a moment when you see yourself stepping into that warrior energy, real or imagined. What could you accomplish if you gave yourself permission to fight all-out for what you believe in and want? What might be the consequences—for you personally, for the political sphere around you, and for the planet?

ake the volcano as a metaphor for your own core, for the passionate energy that bubbles beneath the surface. What do you find when you allow yourself to dive into that molten interior? Describe a specific time when you erupted in passionate furor, be it love, rage or advocacy. What makes you crazy with love or insane with anger? Or if you have never let those deep passions explode, explore: what it is that holds you back?

MAY

The Warmth of Childhood

he Guatemalan Quiché Indian
Rigoberta Menchú won the Nobel
Peace Prize in 1992 for her courageous
human rights work. She went on to
become one of the most important
proponents of the pan-indigenous movement, which
eventually succeeded in winning recognition by the
United Nations of the Universal Declaration of the
Rights of Indigenous Peoples. Menchú describes all
the different human cultures as "kernels on the cob
of humanity"—unique but connected, and not as different as we think we are. We're also much more like
the other life forms of Earth than we are different, all
of us composed from the same basic building blocks
of life: air, water and earth, animated by the Sun.

It seems that we "know" this instinctively in
childhood, when every daisy is delightful, and a
turtle or toad can be your best friend for an afternoon. Children's books celebrate the affinity of

very young humans for the natural world, giving us animals who talk—of course they do!—and landscapes that pulsate with meaning. This month, try to reach back to your childhood self to consider your connections both to other humans and to our larger "tribe" of Gaians. What were your fascinations as a very small child? What were you aware of in the world around you? Step out into your childhood as if you were embarking eagerly on a walk through a landscape vaguely familiar but endlessly new. Who do you meet along the trail? What stories do they have to share with you?

Depending on your circumstances, this exploratory foray into childhood could turn into a romp through a lovely spring wildflower meadow, or a heart-stopping march through a dark threatening forest. Go with it, remembering that now, as you venture back to the terrain of your childhood as a purposeful memoirist, you are in control, and you're here for a reason: to find out how you became who you are today, and what lessons your own experience may have to offer others. Imagine your memoir as a guidebook for others coming along the trail behind you. What knowledge does your childhood self, who still lives on in your memory, need to share with others?

May Catalysts

Earth: Exploring the Connections of Childhood

n the northern hemisphere, the sweet days of May are the heyday of springtime, when the Earth greens, blooms and renews herself again. After the long winter, we all frolic like children in the new grass and sunshine, wishing these spring days would last forever. See if you can remember the first time in your childhood that you were aware of the change of the seasons from winter to spring, and describe what that felt like. Or if you were not aware of seasonal change, describe a moment from your childhood that you wished would never end. In your memory, it doesn't have to! Take us there.

n the first decade of our lives, we develop from infants who know no boundaries between ourselves and our mothers, to children who move with a fair degree of autonomy in the social and physical landscape of our lives. Thinking back to the first ten years of your life, recall one or more moments when you became aware of yourself as part of a larger group of people, whether that identity was religious, ethnic, racial, gender-based or by social class. What shock of recognition accompanied this new awareness of your social connection to a larger identity-based group? Was this discovery pleasing, or was it frightening or unnerving in some way? Describe your entry into one or more of your "social tribes" with as much specificity as you can—even if the truth hurts.

n childhood, even as we're becoming aware of our myriad relationships with other human beings, most of us also become aware of other animals and animate life forms that surround us, be they trees, flowers, animals, fish, birds or insects. What were the special non-human Gaians that populated your childhood years? Did you bond with a pet animal? Feed the pigeons in the park? Or perhaps you grew up on a farm: what was your relationship to the farm animals or the edible landscape surrounding you? Did you have a special climbing tree in childhood, or other particular elements of the landscape that you personified and communicated with? In childhood we are not considered "crazy" when we talk to animals or hug a tree. Try to get back to the simple, direct relationship you had with the non-human landscape of your childhood, and see what relationships with specific Gaians are still alive in your memory.

If you draw a blank and find you did not have such connections to the non-human realm of the planet in childhood, explore why that was so, and how that early estrangement might have affected the child you were—and the adult you have become.

JUNE

Cultivating a Life

une in the northern hemisphere is the time of maximum alertness—the days are long and full, crackling with extra energy from the near-ness of the Sun. It is a good time to reflect on how you project your own energy out into the world. How have you cultivated your own creative potential? What circumstances or people have appeared to boost your efforts and give you wings to soar? What have been the setbacks along the journey to living into your full potential as a human being in this time and place?

This month, give yourself permission to play in your writing. Skip a little! Do a tap-dance and take a bow. Although your memoir is purposeful, it doesn't have to be heavy or serious all the time. Everyone needs to get out and have some fun, and there's no time like the present to break out of your usual routines and try something new. Here are a few suggestions:

✳ Try writing in the second person, using the personal pronoun "you" in place of "I." The slight distance afforded by this linguistic shift can sometimes be surprisingly revealing.

✳ Interview yourself. Come up with some really hard, probing questions, and answer them with as much honesty as you can. Then answer them again, allowing yourself the liberty of lying. Take a break from memoir and write fiction for a change! You can learn a lot about yourself when you put your imagination in the driver's seat.

✳ Stepping away from narrative for a moment, take the time to write an in-depth description of one or more of the most important characters from your memoir. Describe them using as many sensuous details as possible. Show them in action in a scene, with dialogue. Tell the story of who they were before you met them. If you're feeling really daring, let them write to you, telling you just how they feel about you. You can take it—after all, they are a part of you now, just one of the many characters who populate your memories.

Any time your memoir starts to feel too heavy, shift gears and try something different for a while. Remind yourself that you're telling this story for the benefit of others, and to blaze the trail effectively, you need to be the kind of guide who can keep everyone's spirits up. Yes, there will be moments of hardship along the way—do you know anyone who hasn't experienced fear, rage, grief, pain? The essential thing on this elemental journey is to keep moving, knowing that there is a reason your life has unfolded as it has. Part of that reason has to do with sharing what you've learned with others, to help them go forward with more confidence and clarity on their own life journeys.

Human beings have always been tribal, but now, in the 21st century, we are becoming more like our cousins the bees or the termites: hive creatures, tightly networked and interdependent. Think of your memoir as one thread of the intricately woven tapestry of human experience. You are not responsible for the whole—but if each of us gives ourselves with devotion to the warp and woof of our own lives, what a thing of beauty we will create together!

June Catalysts

Air: Looking in the Mirror of the Self

ll of us are born into circumstances quite beyond our control. Like the flowers of the field, we adapt and try to bloom as best we can where we're planted. Look back over your life using the metaphor of cultivating the field of your experience. What field were you born into, in terms of family and culture? To what extent have you been content to continue cultivating yourself within that same field, or how have you struck out to claim and develop new territories of your own? How does your childhood field of experience look from where you are now?

ary Oliver ends one of her most beloved poems, "The Summer Day," with a potent question: "Tell me, what is it you plan to do/with your one wild and precious life?" Taking this question into the realm of the social and political, write your way towards an answer. Do you know what you would like to accomplish in your life? If so, how are you working to achieve these goals? If not, why not? Is this a deliberate choice to "go with the flow," or something else? Write a scene in which you see yourself offering your unique gifts to the world freely and fully, either on an occasion that has already come to pass, or a moment imagined in the future. Pay special attention in your writing to how it *feels* to step into this role.

n the northern hemisphere, the summer Solstice is a time of maximum light and openness. If you could open your heart and mind to allow an unimpeded flow of energy from the core of the planet out into the universe, and from the farthest reaches of the cosmos back down to Earth, what messages might come through you? Imagine yourself as a kind of lightening rod for the great pulses of energy that surround and animate all life. Allowing yourself to speak in the voice of cosmic prophecy, what thundering proclamations or celestial poetry do you hear and convey?

JULY

Learning and Unlearning

s humans, we are born reaching towards what feels good, and hard-wired to learn. Babies quickly learn how to appeal to their caregivers for what they need, and toddlers constantly test the boundaries of acceptable behavior, learning with each instance of positive reinforcement or negative consequences. By the time we're teenagers, we have been through years of education—both informal, from family and friends, and formal, in schools. The challenge becomes how to sort through it all and figure out what thoughts, feelings and actions are in alignment with our deepest, truest selves. What aspects of all we've been taught will we internalize and make a permanent aspect of our personalities? What will we reject?

Depending on the family you've been born into and the schooling you've received, this process may feel easy and natural, or difficult and fraught.

Paulo Freire famously compared conventional education to banking, where knowledge is "deposited" into students' minds, and can be withdrawn on demand, in the form of tests. He advocated shifting to a more dialogic, liberatory form of education—education as a two-way exchange between teachers and students, where both learn and are transformed by the process. This month, think about your most impactful educational experiences as a teenager and young adult. They may have come through school, or out in an alleyway; or maybe you were fortunate enough to have a chance to learn in the great outdoors. They may have been positive or negative experiences—we learn just as much by playing with fire as we do by sitting docilely at a desk. Who were your most important teachers, how did they teach, and what were the lessons that have stayed with you? Perhaps most importantly, what are the lessons that you are now prepared to pass along to the younger ones coming along the path behind you? What do you wish you'd known at their stage of life? What can you share with them now?

July Catalysts

Water: Going with the Flow, Swimming Against the Tide

n the teenage years, we begin to separate from our birth families, define our own identities and seek out our own affinity groups. At the same time, we're being intensively initiated into the norms and expectations of our society through our education, both formal and informal. Looking back at this period in your life, identify a particular scene that tells the story of a moment in which you went along with expectations; and another scene of a time when you made the decision to strike out on your own or with a posse of peers. What did you learn about yourself—and about your social communities—from these experiences? What were the immediate consequences and lasting impacts of the education you received during these years?

s teens and young adults, we begin to become more aware of ourselves as members of various social groups, including religious, ethnic and political affiliations—all of which come with strong sets of norms and rules, both spoken and unspoken. Take stock of the different social communities to which you belonged as a young person, either by birthright or by choice. Write a scene describing yourself in action in the heart of one or more of these communities. How did you feel in this company? What aspects of this social group made you happy, and what caused you unease or grief? Looking back on this period in your life, what principles and beliefs have you gladly taken with you on your journey towards adulthood, and what have you jettisoned along the way as unnecessary baggage?

s a young adult, how tuned in were you to the natural world around you? Were you aware of "the environment" as a site of social struggle and contention over issues like pollution or conservation of land and wildlife? Or did the planet simply form a scenic backdrop for your much-more-interesting social life? Write a scene showing your teenaged or young adult self moving through a typical day on the planet, paying special attention to how you did or did not notice the natural landscape around you.

AUGUST

Reaching for the Light

ugust in New England is a time of shooting stars and fireflies, torrid afternoons rumbling into dramatic thunderstorms and pouring, cooling rain. August is a Fire month, and on the elemental journey, Fire is the stage of adulthood, when we are able to fully embrace our passions, and also when we're challenged by trials and tribulations we could never have anticipated. This month, let's dare to give some thought to the strong emotions of anger and rage that crackle inevitably through our lives. While you may ultimately decide that these emotions do not need to be included in your memoir, it is still a valuable exercise to look squarely at the less savory scenes from your life, and try to discern what life lessons they have taught you. Remember, you are writing purposeful memoir here, which means part of your mission is sharing what you have learned for

the benefit of others who may be experiencing similar circumstances.

So take a deep breath, let it out with a whoosh, and allow yourself to think back over the fiery times in your life, when you were struck by a lightening bolt of misfortune, gripped by fierce rage, or sunk in shame and humiliation. These scenes were hard enough to live through, and they won't be easy to revisit in writing. But if they have been seared into your memory, it's because they were pivotal moments in your growth as a human being. One of Rumi's poems describes how we have to stay open to all the emotions and experiences, even if they're "a crowd of sorrows," because each has something important to teach us. Light enters us through our wounds, Rumi reminds us—but only if we are courageous enough to go through the pain, into the darkness, to reach for that light.

August Catalysts

Fire: Shooting Sparks

nger can be dangerous, as in "a murderous rage," but if focused appropriately, it can also be a tremendously cleansing force. Make a list of times in your life when you have become enraged. Look back over the list and notice patterns: have there been certain people or types of events that have made you angry over the years? Do you tend to experience more anger in certain physical locations? At particular times of year? When you get angry, how do you express your rage? Do you project it at those around you, or boomerang it back in self-destructive behaviors? Take one of the scenes from your list and describe it fully, from the triggering incident, through the explosion of rage, all the way through the lingering aftermath. Do the same with other scenes from the list that seem to be calling out for exploration. Take the time to move through your list thoughtfully and descriptively, sparing no details. Remember, you do not have to share this writing with anyone. But you can learn so much from the exploratory journey.

nger is often justified. All social revolutions and reforms have come about because a group of people got angry and decided not to take it anymore. Looking beyond the personal into the political realm, what injustices or abuses have aroused your righteous anger? What made you decide to join a movement for positive social change, and what happened once you took the plunge? Plunk us down in the center of the swirling energy you experienced as you harnessed anger for social good, and describe everything: where you were, who was there, what was being said, what actions were taken, how it felt to be part of that powerful current. Relive the joy of becoming a *bodhisattva*, a warrior for positive social change, and let us feel the charge with you!

n a planetary level, there is plenty to be angry about these days. As adults, we have to accept some responsibility for having created the fallen world we now lament. Even if we didn't cause the blight ourselves, we may have stood by and allowed to it happen. Let's stand with our feet firmly planted and take a good look at this big globe we call home. What about it pleases you? What makes you angry? What do you hope will continue into the future, and what would you like to change? How can you be part of creating the world you want to leave to your descendants? Is there a place for anger in this vision, as well as for love?

SEPTEMBER

In the Gardens of Memory

here I come from, September is a time of abundance. The farmers' markets are bursting with the fruits of the Earth, and out in the fields the corn tassels wave in the wind and the pumpkins swell big and orange. Writers have often been drawn to the metaphor of the garden to describe our work. We memoirists labor in the fields of memory, bringing in precious harvests from our past. Let's play with that metaphor a bit this month. If your memoir were a garden, what kind of garden would it be? Would it be broad fields of waving wheat, or a carefully plotted English herb garden, complete with climbing roses on the high stone walls? Are you the kind of gardener who tolerates no weeds, or someone who can't bear to pull a dandelion in bloom?

In the garden of purposeful memoir, at least in the early stages of the journey, it doesn't pay to be too fussy. As you work on your crop of focused free-writes, it's best to give free rein to every seed that's planted and any memory that wants to grow, whether it seems weedy and invasive or tidy and neat. Sometimes it's hard to tell at first what the little sprout of a memory might grow into—it could be a dull clump of grass, or it could be a magnificent, monumental sunflower. Give every tendril of memory equal attention and nurturing in the early stages. Let them all flourish. In the end, at harvest-time, you'll be able to see clearly which ones are worth saving and which are better off tossed on the compost heap of personal history, where they'll enrich the beds of our memory for another harvest, another year.

September Catalysts

Earth: Planting, Cultivating, Harvesting...Taking the Longer View

hink about the legacy of your child-
hood and how it still lives within
you, for good or for ill. What experiences of childhood have you
carried within you, like unplanted
seeds that still retain potent untapped potential? If you were to plant and water those seeds
today, what could you imagine growing from
them? Would it be a destructive kudzu vine, a
rare hothouse flower or tough dandelions? Using
a botanical metaphor or not, describe how your
childhood experiences continue to live within
you and influence your life today.

hildren love fairy tales, myths and legends for their simple, bold, black-and-white directness. A princess is good; an ogre is awful; a dragon must be slayed. Or maybe not. Children delight in contradictions, too: the evil princess, the lovable ogre or dragon. Think about the convictions you held in childhood, and how they have changed or stayed the same over the years. What childhood fears have marched along beside you on your life journey, and which have you left behind? If you could address your childhood heroes and demons directly, what kind of conversation might result? What face did Courage wear in your childhood, and how did he speak to you? What about Fear? If you could speak with archetypal emotions and characters from your childhood, what would they say? And how would you respond, given what you know now and who you have become? Go ahead—write those conversations and see what comes!

or most of modern times, we humans have thought of ourselves as marching on a linear evolutionary plane into the future, every step of the journey representing progress towards greater civilization and a higher good. In the 21st century, as we learn more about the full complexity of our planet, and our own place in the intricate ecological web of life, this triumphal procession is looking less like a tree of life, with human beings waving proudly from the topmost branches, and more like a vast spiral. In fact, a recent scientific rendition of the life forms of Earth was conceptualized as a circle, with human beings just one small strand, relatively puny and unimportant compared to the legions of bacteria, microbes, fungi, plants and insects that make up the bulk of life on the planet. Taking a long view of planetary life, we humans are still in our childhood as a species, with plenty of room for growth and development. Each one of us alive today has an important role to play in this evolutionary process. Imagine your life as a link on the long chain of human existence. What valuable qualities do you bring with you from the past—from your own childhood, or from previous generations? What would you like to pass on to your descendants? What could be jettisoned?

OCTOBER

Write Where You Are

irginia Woolf famously insisted that women writers must have "a room of their own" and a steady income to be able to produce fine literature. Some 50 years later, the Chicana writer Gloria Anzaldúa begged to differ, telling would-be writers to "forget the room of one's own," to write on the bus or the toilet seat, to write with "blood and pus and sweat." Both Woolf and Anzaldúa did the best they could with the circumstances they had, producing volumes of work still admired and read today, long after their deaths. Think this month about what conditions help you thrive on your journey of purposeful memoir, and what challenges you face. Do you have a quiet room of your own in which to write? Or do you prefer to write in a crowded, noisy coffee shop? Do you need a good chunk of uninterrupted time to take those long meandering journeys down

memory lane? Or are you the kind of person who does better writing on the fly, perhaps talking your stories into a voice recorder while you drive, or sending yourself quick emails with details you want to remember?

The bottom line is that it doesn't matter where or how you write. It just matters that you do it. How many of us start writing projects we never finish? How many yellowing notebooks are stuffed into drawers with only a few pages written on? How often do we create file folders on our computers but never fill them with documents? Yes, it's true, it's all about the journey; the process is important and valuable even if you never arrive at a finished product. But this month, as we round the corner into the last quarter of the year, take time to look back over what you have written so far and think about your goals and ambitions for this work. What have you accomplished? What remains to be done? How can you give yourself the best possible conditions for your writing life, given the realities of the life you live now?

October Catalysts

Air: Creativity Springs Eternal, in Spite of it All

ver the course of your life, what people, places, events and circumstances have helped you become the person who sits down today, with determination and perseverance, to write? Looking back along the road you've traveled to this moment, what have been the hurdles you've had to overcome? What obstacles still remain to your full realization of your intention to write down the stories of your life? Describe a moment when you have been most engaged and productive—not necessarily at writing, but at any creative endeavor. What were the conditions that made this moment possible, and how might you be able to recreate them in the future?

irginia Woolf, that bard of the feminine spirit, wrote famously of Shakespeare's sister, who was just as gifted as her brother but never had a chance to develop or present her talents, because she was born female in a time that refused to recognize, cultivate or reward talented creative women. In our time and place there are still gatekeepers and naysayers, discouraging, if not outright forbidding, certain people from bringing their creative gifts fully into the world. Have there been any such negative forces at work in your life, dampening your ambition, undermining your confidence, preventing you from stepping boldly and gaily into the creative arena? If so, now is your moment to stand up and fight back! Nod politely to every person or circumstance that bars your path, set them aside and walk proudly on by. You are your own best cheerleader and pit crew—you don't need permission from others to make your creative dreams come true. You just need a certain amount of grit and persistence, a good dose of hard work, and the buoyancy of a creative vision that will grow clearer and more vivid the more you contemplate and work with it. This is your time, and you are the one we've all been waiting for. Go do it!

ertain places on the planet are said to have special resonance, whether because of their ley lines or quartz crystals, their deep caves or high mountains, their crashing waves or dark lush jungles. Imagine that you could take yourself anywhere on Earth to set up a writing camp. Where on the planet would you write best? Describe your surroundings: your writing perch and implements; the people who are (or are not) around you. After you've described the place thoroughly, sit yourself down in the center of your creation, make yourself comfortable, and write. What comes?

NOVEMBER

Veils Between Worlds

ovember is the witching month, when the veils between the physical and metaphysical worlds are thin—in the northern hemisphere, ghosts walk abroad for Halloween and the Day of the Dead, as the year slowly pivots on its axis towards the dark months of winter. Let's think about the ghosts in your family history this month. The new science of epigenetics has established what many of us always suspected: that the experiences of our ancestors, whether positive or negative, can actually affect and change our DNA. Ancient, cellular-level memories of terror can make us inexplicably fearful; and joyful experiences also imprint themselves on us in a lightness of spirit and sunny optimism that can pass along the generations.

It is well worth the time and effort to do some research on your family history, even if it's not immediately apparent how this history will become part of your memoir. Trace your lineages as far back as you can, trying to uncover not only the facts of your ancestors' lives, but their dreams and aspirations, their ethics and passions, the way they ran their households, raised their children and lived day-to-day. You're sure to uncover some resonances that surprise you, along with, perhaps, some qualities or patterns that you recognize all too well. You may even discover some aspects of your ancestors that embarrass or upset you; truths that you'll wish you didn't have to know. But you got yourself into memoir because you're curious about the reality of your life, and your family is deeply a part of you, their cells alive in yours. Knowing about their lives can help you understand your own. So this month, let those ghosts walk. Take out your pad and jot down some notes as they tell you about themselves. And then think deeply about how they live on—in you.

November Catalysts

Water: Charting the
Flow of Time

magine yourself as a link in a long chain of people, stretching back into the past and forward into the future. Make a list of the qualities and tendencies you carry with you from your matrilineal line. Now do the same for your patrilineal line. Looking at the list, which qualities and tendencies do you embrace and feel grateful for, and which would you like to jettison? Thinking of your own life and life story as a link, made tangible and readable, between past and future, what are the strengths and positive qualities you hope to pass on, whether literally or figuratively, to the future? Taking this imaginative journey through history a little further, write some letters this month:

* A letter to you from your great-great-great-grandmother, written when she was a teenager or young adult, with her whole life before her (first figure out what year she might have written this letter, and imagine her in her historical time and place);

* A letter from you in response;

* A letter to you from your great-great-great-granddaughter (or another related descendant, if you do not have children of your own); again, calculate the year of her birth, and imagine her as a teenager or young adult, letting her tell you, in the letter, about her life and times;

* A letter from you in response.

emoir is always about more than just the personal. In fact, by writing memoir we discover just how political the personal always is. Take some time to create a timeline of your life (possibly including your parents' and grandparents' generations as well). On the top of the line, note historical incidents that had some impact on you or your family—wars, economic ups or downs, social movements, political changes, etc. On the bottom of the line, chart the more personal, intimate incidents of importance—weddings, births, deaths, moves, job changes, financial struggles or successes, and so on. Once your timeline is completed, do some deep process writing about what you find there. How do the official history and the personal history of you and your family intertwine? What do you understand better about yourself or your family by understanding the social and historical backdrop of your individual lives?

nd then there's the planet, our beautiful battered old Gaia. What happens if you add another level to your timeline, charting planetary history? It is fascinating to realize just how short and insignificant a century is in the deep history of geological time. But take the past century as a timeframe, and do some research, if necessary, about what has happened to the phys-ical Earth and the non-human life forms with whom we share our planet. You can start with your own town or county: how has it changed in the past hundred years? Then move out further in space: how has your state changed? Your country? Your hemisphere? What people or creatures used to live here that are no longer present? How have changes in the built and natural landscape affected the lives of you and your ancestors over the past century? What has been gained, and what has been lost?

DECEMBER

Taking Stock of the Journey

s the calendar year draws to a close, we in the northern hemisphere light candles, kindle fires and come together to share holiday cheer as a bulwark against the cold darkness outside. In the old days, before electricity kept us running like gerbils on a treadmill year-round, December was a time to slow down and settle in for long winter naps, or storytelling sessions around the fire. It's a good time to pause and reflect on how your memoir has developed since you began working on it, whether that was a few months or a few years ago.

One dark evening this month, light yourself a candle, take out your notebook, and do some process writing just for yourself. Thinking back through all your writing to date, what scenes stand out the most strongly? What little seedlings of memory still need more tending? What memories have you been reluctant to dive into, afraid, perhaps, of what the exploration will reveal? What has surprised you, so far, along this elemental journey? Are you starting to understand your larger purpose in writing this memoir? Can you explain it, at least to yourself?

December Catalysts

Fire: Return to Light

hinking back over your life, what people, places or events have brought you alive, giving you the freedom and lightness of spirit you need to express your full creative potential? Take some time this month to write one or more of these enlivening scenes fully, in rich detail. Then look into the future and ask yourself seriously: how can I bring more of this enlivenment into my life?

hinking about yourself in relation to your generation, how would you characterize your connection with the general zeitgeist of your time and place? Do you fit right in and march to the predominant beat? Or have you often found yourself sitting on the sidelines watching others play the game? Or maybe you are dancing somewhere off by yourself, or with a few kindred spirits? Do some writing this month about your relationship to the different communities you are part of, from your family to your workplace, clubs or religious groups, political parties, nationality and even ethnicity, class, race or gender. How do you define yourself, and how do others define you? How well does your self-understanding match the way others see you? Are you content with this correspondence (or lack thereof)? Or is it something you'd like to address as you move into the future?

ull the darkness of the Northern Hemisphere of the planet around you like a cozy cocoon. In your sweet moments of solitude, what transformative visions are you weaving? A caterpillar must dissolve entirely to be reborn as a butterfly. What are you sloughing off in this period of deep reflection, and what will you carry with you as you move forward into the New Year, towards the light?

CONCLUSION

Be Your Note:
Continuing on the Elemental
Journey of Purposeful Memoir

Be Your Note:
Continuing on the Elemental
Journey of Purposeful Memoir

reud famously compared memory to
the city of Pompeii, with ruins and
artifacts buried in layers on the same
ground, the strata marking different
epochs. But for the 21st century memoirist, a better analogy can be drawn from quantum
theory: in your mind, different scenes from the past
are all constantly playing out in parallel universes
that you can access anytime through the power of
your memory and imagination. Picture your memory
like a long hallway, lined with lots of doors on both
sides, like the corridor of a big hotel. Each door leads
into a specific time and place from your past, and
you can go into any one and pick up in that moment
as if you'd never left. Seen this way, the process of
writing memoir becomes a fascinating game: which
door will you open tonight? Generally it's best not
to overthink it—just walk along in your imagination,
open a door, and see where you are. Then describe

what you see—are you inside or outside? Alone or with others? What is happening in that moment? What are you feeling and thinking? Write it down!

Once you've accumulated what feels to you like a substantial amount of writing, print it all out (if you've been working on a computer) and read it through carefully. Don't give the editor-imp too much leeway in pointing out everything that's wrong; you're not here to sabotage your writing, you're here to nurture and cultivate it! Here are a few things you should look for, as the first reader of your own work (these questions can also be used by writing group members, for each other):

* Are the principal characters in your stories thoroughly described and developed? Do we know enough about them—what they look like, how they speak, what they like to do in their free time, where they live, etc.—to be able to imagine them in our mind's eye? If not, keep writing!

* Have you included dialogue in your scenes? Even if you don't remember the precise words used, recreating a dialogue from your memory is perfectly acceptable in memoir, and if you can capture your characters' vernacular or odd turns of phrase, it will help them come alive for your readers.

✳ Have you thoroughly described the places your memoir takes us to? Remember to include as many senses as possible in your descriptions—sound and smell can be as important to the spirit of a place as vision.

✳ Is your writing compelling? Novice writers can sometimes fall into the trap of over-writing—using too many adverbs and adjectives in an attempt to be thorough. The best rule of thumb is to write simply, directly and with just a tad more descriptive color than you might use in telling the same story to your best friend.

✳ Is the narrative thread clear within each scene, and between scenes? In other words, are we able to follow the story's plot and timeline?

After you've read through your work, settle in to do some serious process writing about it. Take your time and be thoughtful in answering the key questions that follow. These are questions you may need to return to more than once, as your memoir slowly takes shape.

Catalysts for Process Writing
On Your Memoir Draft

✳ What periods of your life or stories from your life are you finding most interesting and compelling today?

✳ What is the narrative timeline of your memoir: where does the big arc of your story start, where does it end, and what are the important signposts or watershed moments along the way that must be included?

✳ What is the deep vein of memory you're interested in mining further?

✳ What patterns, themes or guiding questions are starting to emerge?

✳ How do you see your personal experience connecting to or being informed by family history as well as official history and larger societal trends and circumstances?

There are a few issues that are so important to memoir, particularly purposeful memoir, that they deserve more than a bullet point. The first one has to do with the question of time. To construct a memoir, you will have to decide whether you are going to simply move forward chronologically, starting in the past and ending somewhere closer to the present; or whether you're going to employ a more complex structure, perhaps starting in the present and using flashbacks to explore the past. There are endless ways to handle time in a memoir, but it's important for you to know where you stand, temporally speaking, as the narrator. Are you going to use the power of hindsight? In other words, when you describe your childhood, are you going to do so with all the knowledge you have accumulated as an adult? Or are you going to try to recreate, as nearly as possible, the mindset you had as a little child? This decision has big implications for how you'll describe the people and events of your childhood. For instance, perhaps you didn't realize, as a child, that your father was an alcoholic. Will you describe him the way you saw him then, as someone whose behavior was strangely erratic? Or will you give him the label your adult perspective can now identify? There is no right or wrong way to go here, but as you continue to work on the memoir, you should be conscious of the decisions you're making along the way, and aim for accuracy and consistency.

Talking about the real live people who have shown up in your life story brings up some tricky issues for memoirists. On the one hand, this is *your* story, and you have every right to tell it from your own perspective, as it feels right to you. On the other hand, most of us don't want to hurt people we love—or people we have loved—by telling stories that don't show them in their best light. As you move towards sharing your memoir more widely, beyond the small circle of writing partners you have already enjoined to confidentiality, you will need to think carefully about your portraits of living people (and even, to some extent, your ancestor portraits, since their other descendants have some stake in how these family ghosts are portrayed). First of all, be sure you're telling the truth as you see it. Or if you're bending the truth, be aware of it, and comfortable with your motives. If you are going to be critical of a living person in your memoir, be sure you understand libel law and protect yourself accordingly. Changing names "to protect the privacy of individuals" is always an option, as is publishing under a pseudonym. If you are dealing with really radioactive material, you might have to consider shifting from memoir to fiction; the hybrid designation "autobiographical novel" is a common way out of this dilemma.

As I said at the outset of our journey together in this book, it's best not to censor yourself in the beginning. Let all your stories out, and tell them as truthfully as you can bear to. But once you've amassed a good deal of material, and are beginning to have a sense of how this pile of focused free-writes might one day become a book, you should be clear-eyed and thoughtful about the impact of your story on others who have shared life experiences with you. Be sure you know your purpose in telling these particular stories. Purposeful memoir will sometimes demand that we move beyond our own comfort zones because we have a story to share that will help others in similar circumstances. If this is the case for you, look into your own heart, listen deeply, and do what you think is right. Talk over your decisions with your writing partner or group, and eventually with an editor as well. Especially with memoir, we are so close to our own stories that after a while we can't see our own work clearly. Once you have what you consider to be a full rough draft, a skilled editor will be invaluable; with her outsider's eye, she can take that hunk of marble—your rough draft—and whittle it away deftly to reveal the stunning statue that had been waiting inside for the invitation to take form.

But that will come later. For now, another important question to consider is: for whom are you writing? If you simply want to record your life story or family history for your grandchildren, then it's easy to identify your ideal reader: it's your favorite grandchild, of course! But if you are interested in reaching a wider audience with your memoir, then you need to think more deeply about how the issues important to your life intersect with the experiences of others. Start by making a list of the categories of people who might be interested in your memoir because some aspect of your experience overlaps with theirs. For example, people born in the 1950s, divorcées, people whose children have died, women politicians, dog fanciers—relate the highlights of your memoir to groups of people who will be intrigued by your story because their lives too have been touched by similar circumstances or interests. One or more of these groups are your "target audience," to slip into the jargon of publishing.

Once you know your ideal reader, take the time to a) describe him or her thoroughly in writing; and then b) write a nice friendly letter to this person, explaining in detail why you think your story will interest them. Out of this letter, see if you can take the next step of boiling down your description of your memoir into one sentence—the sentence on the back cover that will convince your ideal reader, who has picked up your book in the bookstore one day, that they must buy and read it immediately. Because this is what you want to write, isn't it? A must-read book. A memoir that shares the lessons life has taught you because they will be of value to others as well.

Rumi imagines each human being as a flute through which God blows a unique note. Think deeply about this metaphor and ask yourself: what is the note that has been blowing through me since childhood? Has the tone changed over the years? What note do I want to leave resounding in the minds of my readers?

There is no right or wrong note, Rumi says. All that is asked of us is to be our note.

Elemental Journey
Correspondences

Zodiac sign	Calendar period	Element
Capricorn	12/21 – 1/19	EARTH
Aquarius	1/20 – 2/18	AIR
Pisces	2/10 – 3/20	WATER
Aries	3/21 – 4/20	FIRE
Taurus	4/21- 5/20	EARTH
Gemini	5/21 – 6/20	AIR
Cancer	6/21 – 7/20	WATER
Leo	7/21 – 8/21	FIRE
Virgo	8/22 – 9/22	EARTH
Libra	9/23 – 10/22	AIR
Scorpio	10/23 – 11/22	WATER
Sagittarius	11/23 – 12/20	FIRE

SUGGESTIONS FOR FURTHER READING

Purposeful memoirs

Anzaldúa, Gloria. *Borderlands/la frontera: The New Mestiza*. 1987.

Ehrenreich, Barbara. *Living with a Wild God*. 2014.

Ensler, Eve. *In the Body of the World: A Memoir of Cancer and Connection*. 2014.

Hill, Julia Butterfly. *The Legacy of Luna: The Story of a Woman, a Tree and the Struggle to Save the Redwoods*. 2001.

Hogan, Linda. *The Woman Who Watches Over the World: A Native Memoir*. 2002.

Lorde, Audre. *Zami: A New Spelling of My Name*. 1982.

Maathai, Wangari. *Unbowed: A Memoir*. 2007.

Miranda, Deborah. *Bad Indians: A Tribal Memoir*. 2013.

Partnoy, Alicia. *The Little School: Tales of Disappearance and Survival*. 1986.

Steingraber, Sandra. *Living Downstream: An Ecologist's Personal Investigation of Cancer and the Environment*. 1997.

Williams, Terry Tempest. *Refuge: An Unnatural History of Family and Place*. 1992.

Writing Advice

Aronie, Nancy Slonim. *Writing from the Heart*. 1998.

Elbow, Peter. *Writing Without Teachers*. 1953.

Gilbert, Elizabeth. *Big Magic: Creative Living Beyond Fear*. 2015.

Goldberg, Natalie. *Old Friend From Far Away: The Practice of Writing Memoir*. 2002.

   – *Writing Down the Bones: Freeing the Writer Within*. 1986.

King, Stephen. *On Writing: A Memoir of Craft*. 2000.

Lamott, Ann. *Bird by Bird: Some Instructions on Writing and Life*. 1995.

Pipher, Mary. *Writing to Change the World*. 2007.

Shapiro, Dani. *Still Writing: The Perils and Pleasures of a Creative Life*. 2014.

William Zinsser, ed. *Inventing the Truth: The Art and Craft of Memoir*. 1998.

ACKNOWLEDGMENTS

My style of teaching writing owes much to the Bard Institute for Writing and Thinking. I am grateful to writing teachers Natalie Harper, Jamie Hutchinson and Joan DelPlato, who taught me and other faculty members so much when they spearheaded the Writing & Thinking Workshop at Bard College at Simon's Rock. I also learned a great deal from working for many years alongside my colleague and writing partner Cindy Parrish.

Thanks to my publishing and teaching partner Jana Laiz, as well as to all my friends and sister writers of the Berkshire Festival of Women Writers, a writing community dedicated to providing the nurturing and encouragement we all need to take ourselves seriously as emerging writers.

A big shout-out to my students, especially the memoirists who have taken my workshops—this book is for you.

Jennifer Browdy
Bush Island, Nova Scotia
June 2016

Photo by Jake Borden

Jennifer Browdy

ABOUT THE AUTHOR

Jennifer Browdy is a writer, teacher, community organizer and public speaker with many years of experience teaching memoir and creative non-fiction at the college level.

The founding director of the Berkshire Festival of Women Writers, a collaborative working to nourish and celebrate the voices and visions of women and girls, she is the editor of three anthologies of contemporary writing by women from Latin America, the Caribbean, Africa and North America.

The author of a memoir, *What I Forgot...and Why I Remembered: A Journey to Environmental Awareness and Activism Through Purposeful Memoir*, Jennifer frequently leads writing workshops for adults and teens, taking special delight in leading other women down the endlessly fascinating path of purposeful memoir.

For more information on Jennifer's lectures, workshops, author coaching and editing, visit JenniferBrowdy.com.

WHAT I
FORGOT

...AND WHY I REMEMBERED

A Journey to
Environmental Awareness and Activism
Through Purposeful Memoir

JENNIFER BROWDY

You may also enjoy:

What I Forgot...
And Why I Remembered

*A Journey to Environmental Awareness and
Activism Through Purposeful Memoir*

**What I Forgot...And Why I Remembered is a
must-read for anyone interested in undertaking
the inner work necessary for effective activism.**

This lyrical, hard-hitting memoir sets one Amer-
ican woman's journey against the larger landscape
of political upheaval, global climate change, and the
recovery of our primary connection to the Earth. In
telling the story of a generation who "forgot" how
important the health of our planet is to our personal
health and well-being, Jennifer Browdy details her
own years of being entranced, both personally and
professionally, in patterns of denial and avoidance.
Honestly interrogating the challenge of getting privi-
leged Americans to wake up and confront the urgent
and uncomfortable realities of our time, she calls on
readers to begin the process of transformation at the
intersection of the personal, political and planetary.

Available now from Green Fire Press
Greenfirepress.com

Made in the USA
Columbia, SC
27 August 2018